43.8

MORTON COUNTY LIBRARY

66925

W9-BYW-307

WITHDRAWN FROM
COLLECTION

DRAW
THE
TITANIC

DRAW THE TITANIC

Hulton Deutsch/Corbis

Written by Andrew Staiano

Illustrated by Jason Pederson

SCHOLASTIC INC.

New York Toronto London Auckland Sydney
Mexico City New Delhi Hong Kong

No part of this publication may be reproduced in whole or in part, or stored in a retrieval system, or transmitted in any form or by any means, electronic, mechanical, photocopying, recording, or otherwise, without written permission of the publisher. For information regarding permission, write to Tangerine Press, 1080 Greenwood Blvd., Lake Mary, FL 32779.

ISBN 0-439-07670-6

Copyright © 1998 by NTC/Contemporary Publishing Group, Inc. and Tangerine Press. All rights reserved. Published by Scholastic Inc., 555 Broadway, New York, NY 10012, by arrangement with Tangerine Press. SCHOLASTIC and associated logos are trademarks and/or registered trademarks of Scholastic Inc.

12 11 10 9 8 7 6 5 4 3 2   8 9/9 0 1 2 3/0

Printed in the U.S.A.

First Scholastic printing, November 1998

CONTENTS

DRAWING TIPS

This book shows you how to draw the *Titanic* and other related people and objects. There are many different ways to draw, but here are just a few tips that every aspiring artist should know!

 Each illustration includes step-by-step instructions to help you as you draw. Keep in mind that the final step features only one way the drawing can be finished. Use your imagination to finish each drawing as you wish.

 Use a large sheet of paper and make your drawing fill up the space. That way, it's easy to see what you are doing, and it will give you plenty of room to add details.

 When you are blocking in large shapes, draw by moving your whole arm, not just your fingers or your wrist.

 Experiment with different kinds of lines: Do a light line, then gradually bear down for a wider, darker one. You'll find that just by changing the thickness of a line, your whole picture will look different! Also, try groups of lines, drawing all the lines straight, crisscrossed, curved, or jagged.

 Remember that every artist has his or her own style. That's why the pictures you draw won't look exactly like the ones in the book. Instead, they'll reflect your own creative touch.

 Most of all, have fun!

WHAT YOU'LL NEED

PAPER

Many kinds of paper can be used for drawing, but some are better than others. For pencil drawing, avoid newsprint or rough paper because they don't erase well. Instead, use a large pad of bond paper (or a similar type). The paper doesn't have to be thick, but it should be uncoated, smooth, and cold pressed. You can find bond paper at an art store. If you are using ink, a dull-finished, coated paper works well.

PENCILS, CHARCOAL, AND PENS

A regular school pencil is fine for the drawings in this book, but try to use one with a soft lead. Pencils with a soft lead are labeled #2; #3 pencils have a hard lead. If you want a thicker lead, ask an art store clerk or your art teacher for an artist's drafting pencil.

Charcoal works well when you want a very black line, so if you're just starting to draw with charcoal, use a charcoal pencil of medium to hard grade. Use it to rub in shadows, then erase certain areas to make highlights. Work with large pieces of paper, as charcoal is difficult to control in small drawings. And remember that charcoal smudges easily!

If you want a smooth, thin ink line, try a rolling-point or a fiber-point pen. Art stores and bigger stationery stores have them in a variety of line widths and fun, bright colors.

If you are drawing on colored paper, you may want to experiment with a white pastel pencil. It creates bright highlights when combined with a black pen or a charcoal pencil.

ERASERS

An eraser is one of your most important tools! Besides removing unwanted lines and cleaning up smudges, erasers can be used to make highlights and textures. Get a soft plastic type (the white ones are good), or for very small areas, a gray kneaded eraser can be helpful. Try not to take off ink with an eraser because it will ruin the drawing paper. If you must take an ink line out of your picture, use liquid whiteout.

OTHER HANDY TOOLS

Facial tissues are helpful for creating soft shadows—just go over your pencil marks with a tissue, gently rubbing the area you want smoothed out.

A square of metal window screen is another tool that can be used to make shadows. Hold it just above your paper and rub a soft pencil lead across it. Then rub the shavings from the pencil into the paper to make a smooth, shadowed area in your picture. If you like, you can sharpen the edge of the shadow with your eraser.

You will also need a pencil sharpener, but if you don't have one, rub a small piece of sandpaper against the side of your pencil to keep the point sharp.

FINISHING YOUR DRAWING

As you'll see with the figures and objects in this book, artists can use different drawing techniques to make their pictures unique. Here are some useful techniques for giving your drawings style and personality.

HATCHING

Hatching is a group of short, straight lines used to create a texture or a shadow. When you curve the hatching lines, you create a rounded look. This is handy when texturing a boat's curved body or underside, as shown here with the lifeboat. When you draw the hatching lines close together, you create a dark shadow. For very light shading, draw the lines shorter, thinner, and farther apart.

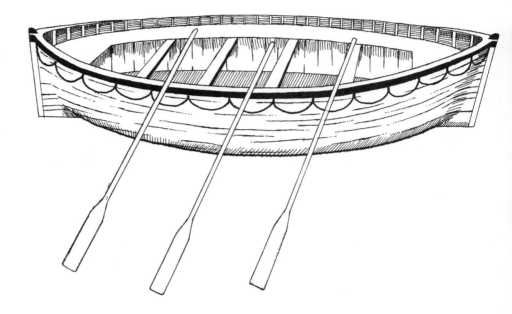

CROSS-HATCHING

This technique gives your drawing an even more shaded look. Start with an area of hatching, then crisscross it with a new set of lines. Compare this picture to the hatching drawing above to see how cross-hatching creates darker shadows and texture. See how cross-hatching has been used on the inside of the crow's nest and on the crewman?

STIPPLE

When you want to give your drawing a different feel, try the stipple technique—and all you need are dots! This method works best with a pen, because unlike a pencil, a pen will make an even black dot just by touching the paper.

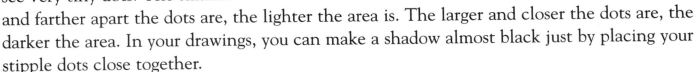

The stipple technique is very similar to the way photos are printed in newspapers and books. If you look through a magnifying glass at a picture in a newspaper, you will see very tiny dots. The smaller and farther apart the dots are, the lighter the area is. The larger and closer the dots are, the darker the area. In your drawings, you can make a shadow almost black just by placing your stipple dots close together.

SMOOTH TONE

By using the side of your pencil, you can create a smooth texture on your drawing, shown here. Starting with the areas you want to be light, stroke the paper very lightly and evenly. Put a little bit more pressure on your pencil as you move to the areas you want to be darker. If you want an area even smoother, go back and rub the pencil with a facial tissue, but rub gently! If you get smudges in areas you want to stay white, simply remove them with an eraser.

Now that you're armed with the basic drawing tools and techniques, you're ready to get started on the drawings in this book, which are on pages 22 through 59. Throughout this book, you can use the techniques that are shown with each of the drawings, or you can make up your own—it's up to you!

MORTON MANDAN PUBLIC LIBRARY

THE VOYAGE OF THE *TITANIC*

The *Titanic* was launched from Southampton, England, at noon on April 10, 1912. It stopped in Cherbourg, France, and Queenstown, Ireland; then, on April 11, it cast off for New York, its final destination. The *Titanic* should have reached New York on April 17, 1912; however, three days after leaving Ireland, the "unsinkable" ship hit an iceberg. Within hours, it sank to the bottom of the North Atlantic Ocean.

The *Titanic* was discovered in 1985 by Robert D. Ballard and Jean-Louis Michel at 41°43'45" North Latitude and 49°56'50" West Longitude, about 400 miles southeast of the Canadian Island of Newfoundland.

DID YOU KNOW . . .

that the *Titanic* almost did not make it out of England's port?

While the Titanic was moving out of port, it created a huge wake that snapped the ropes holding in another ship. The stern of the ship swung out toward the Titanic, nearly hitting it. A nearby tugboat attached a line to the other ship and pulled it away while the Titanic reversed its engines and steered backward. Ironically, the name of the ship the Titanic almost hit was the New York, the port the Titanic was supposed to have reached.

The Titanic *departs Southampton, England, April 10, 1912.*

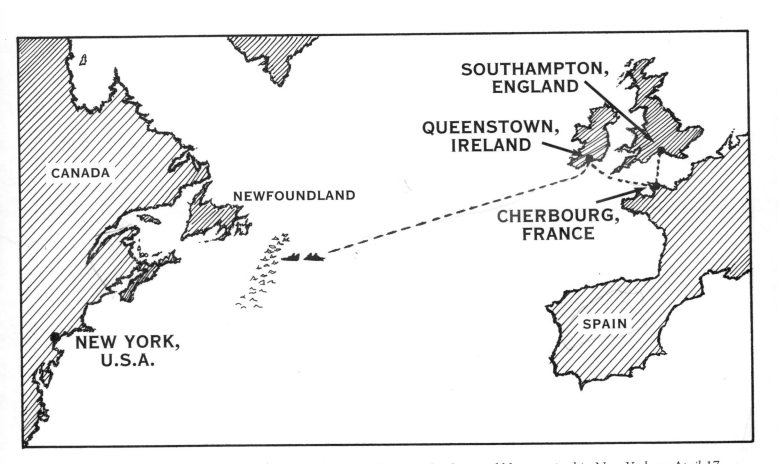

This map shows the Titanic's *path. If the trip had gone as planned, the ship would have arrived in New York on April 17.*

THE R.M.S. TITANIC

The *Titanic* was one of the largest ships ever made. Built in Belfast, Ireland, by Harland and Wolff for the American White Star Line, it was designed to compete with the ships of other commercial passenger cruise lines. Harland and Wolff was the world's most expensive shipbuilder, but the White Star Line wanted the best. It took over a year to finish the *Titanic*. At its completion in 1912, the ship was over 882 feet long and 92 feet wide with nine decks. As tall as an eleven-story building, the *Titanic* weighed over 50,000 tons (as much as 7,500 elephants!).

The *Titanic* was held together with three million rivets. Each of its four smokestacks was wide enough to drive two trains through. The *Titanic* needed three propellers to drive the massive ship through the water. The middle propeller measured 16 feet across, and the others measured over 23 feet. The two *Titanic* anchors, each weighing more than 15 tons, were built a short distance from where the hull was being completed. It took twenty horses to pull just one anchor to the ship. The *Titanic* was indeed, as some newspapers called it, "the wonder ship."

The *Titanic* was able to carry 3,547 people. Advertised as "the last word in luxury," it contained a gymnasium, Turkish baths, an indoor swimming pool, and a squash court. It even had kennels for the passengers' pets and a crewman assigned to walk the guests' dogs every day! Millionaires such as John Jacob Astor, who was probably the world's richest man, Isidor Straus, the founder of Macy's, and mining machinery manufacturer Benjamin Guggenheim dined on the finest foods in the plush Café Parisienne. There the first-class passengers chatted about their accommodations, as well as the fine automobiles and other treasures they were bringing to the United States. After dinner, first-class passengers listened to the ragtime music played in the

The majestic Titanic, *ready for its maiden voyage.*

AP/Wide World Photos

first-class reception room at the base of the grand staircase. Others with first-class tickets enjoyed the world's finest cigars in the smoking room.

Not everyone on board the *Titanic* was privileged enough to enjoy the luxuries the ship had to offer. An important characteristic of the time was the separation of people into classes based on their background, education, and wealth. First-class passengers, the very wealthy, had their own section of the ship, which second- and third-class passengers were not allowed to enter. Second-class passengers, including mostly teachers, shop owners, and professionals, were able to afford a comfortable lifestyle but were not wealthy by any means. Third-class passengers came from many different countries, hoping to start a new life in the United States. Most of them probably spent all the money they had on a one-way ticket to America.

Second- and third-class passengers' rooms were small and lacked the comforts of the first-class staterooms. The typical third-class room consisted of four bunk beds, a dresser, and a washbasin. The second-class room typically had two bunk beds, a dresser, two washbasins, and perhaps a cabinet in which to hang clothes, or a sofa that provided an extra sleeping area. The second- and third-class rooms were far more comfortable than those of other ships at the time. Third-class passengers were used to riding in the cargo hold with the luggage.

The first-class staterooms were nothing short of magnificent. Some of these rooms contained a coal-burning fireplace, a four-poster bed, a writing desk, marble washbasins, a few dressers, and a sofa. Thick carpets covered the floors, and ornate wood paneling and artwork decorated the walls.

DID YOU KNOW . . .
the *Titanic* was equipped with state-of-the-art technology?

Although the telegraph and telephone were both relatively new and expensive means of communication, they were needed to operate such a giant ship. From the wheelhouse, the Titanic's navigators telegraphed messages to the crewmen in the engine rooms, telling them to increase or decrease the amount of coal they were shoveling into the boilers. In addition, lookouts from the crow's nest telephoned officers on the bridge when an iceberg was spotted.

Passengers also benefited from this technology, as they could send telegraphic messages to relatives at home. It is possible that the Titanic's radio operators were so busy with the passengers' messages that they may have missed some early iceberg warnings from nearby ships.

The second- and third-class passengers ate simple meals—perhaps soup, followed by corned beef and cabbage, potatoes, and bread. These meals were quite different from the lobster, roast beef, and champagne enjoyed by the first-class passengers!

Second- and third-class passengers could not enjoy the gymnasium, the Turkish baths, or the swimming pool. Instead, they gathered in the general room and wrote letters to relatives, read books, or sang songs. Third-class children played on the big cranes that were used to lift first-class passengers' cargo on board. These cranes were located on the second- and third-class deck areas, directly above the cargo holds.

Captain Edward J. Smith

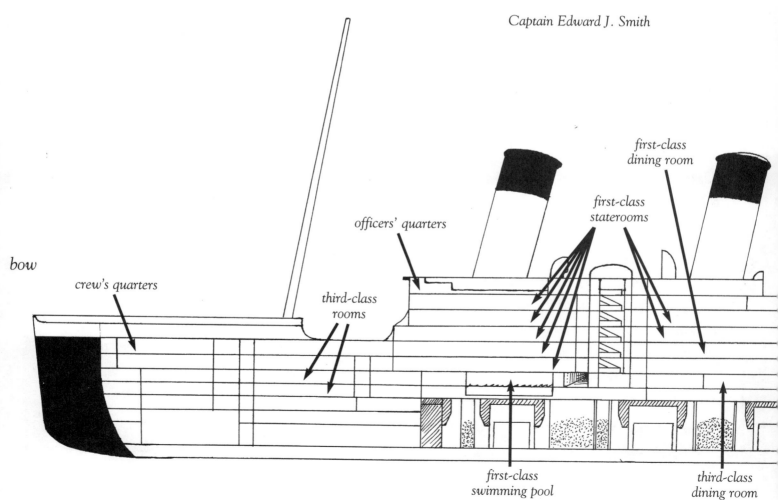

bow

crew's quarters

third-class rooms

officers' quarters

first-class staterooms

first-class dining room

first-class swimming pool

third-class dining room

The crew of the *Titanic* worked very hard to keep the ship running smoothly for its guests. Captain Edward J. Smith and his officers commanded the *Titanic* from the bridge. The chefs in the many kitchens prepared over 4,000 meals a day. In the cargo hold, it is estimated that there was enough food to feed the inhabitants of a small town, including approximately 40,000 fresh eggs, 7,000 heads of lettuce, 36,000 apples, and over 2,000 bags of potatoes. In the boiler rooms, at the bottom of the ship, crewmen worked long, hard hours throwing coal into the boilers in order to keep the *Titanic*'s giant steam engines running. These boilers stood over 15 feet high. In fact, it was one of these giant boilers, unique to the *Titanic*, that helped those searching for the ship to identify it correctly on the ocean floor.

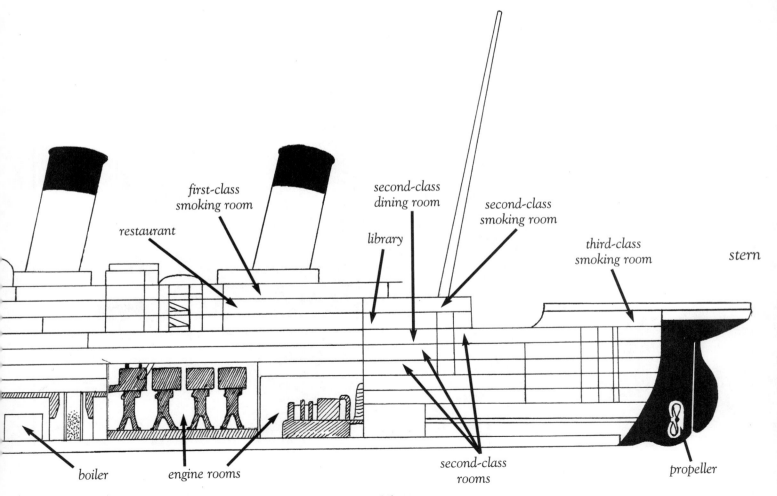

first-class
smoking room

restaurant

second-class
dining room

library

second-class
smoking room

third-class
smoking room

stern

boiler

engine rooms

second-class
rooms

propeller

THE FATEFUL NIGHT

April 14, 1912. The *Titanic* was steaming near full speed on a calm sea. Captain Smith had just finished attending a dinner party with a few first-class guests when he went straight to the bridge, where he found out that there had been another iceberg warning. Captain Smith had read several iceberg warnings that day but wasn't overly concerned about them. He had been a seaman for nearly thirty years and was commanding the *Titanic*, "the unsinkable ship." Still, he thought it would be wise to discuss the situation with his officers. Captain Smith knew that it was more difficult to spot icebergs on a calm sea because there were no waves to crash against them. Also, the moonless night made it extremely difficult to see the waters ahead. He warned the officers to be more alert than usual and then retired to his quarters.

At about 11:40 P.M., one of the lookouts in the crow's nest high above the ship spotted a huge mass off in the distance. He immediately sounded the alarm bell three times and called the bridge. "Iceberg right ahead!" he shouted into the telephone. The officer on the bridge gave an order for the wheel to be turned as far as it would go in order to avoid the mountain of ice. Then he telegraphed the crew in the engine room to reverse the engines. A few seconds later, the starboard bow of the *Titanic* scraped the side of the iceberg. They had avoided a head-on collision but could not miss the iceberg entirely. Several tons of ice crashed onto the deck of the ship. The officer on the bridge pushed the button to seal the doors between the watertight

compartments at the bottom of the ship. A few minutes later, as the *Titanic*'s engines stopped, started again, and then stopped for the last time, an eerie silence overcame the night.

Passengers came out of their rooms to see what had happened. As the ship took on water, crewmen worked frantically to move luggage and mail to higher ground. Captain Smith went down below with Thomas Andrews, the *Titanic*'s builder, to inspect the damage. Five of the ship's sixteen watertight compartments were already flooded. Because they were not sealed at the top, it was only a matter of time before the compartments would all be flooded, ensuring that the *Titanic* would sink. Andrews told the captain that the ship would probably last no more than an hour and a half.

The officer on the bridge ordered the ship's white distress flares to be fired. He could see the lights of a ship off in the distance, but that ship never responded. Captain Smith ordered the wireless operator to send out the regulation international distress call, the Morse code "CQD." Smith then left the radio room to order that the lifeboats be uncovered. When he returned to the radio room to check on responses to the distress call, Harold Bride, the First Wireless

Operator's assistant, suggested they try using the new "SOS" signal that was just coming into use. It was much easier to recognize than "CQD" and easier to send out. Several ships responded to the distress calls. Of the ones that responded, the ship closest to the *Titanic*, the *Carpathia*, was approximately 58 miles away and reported that it was rushing to the rescue. But how long would it take to arrive on the scene?

Up on deck, passengers were being ordered into lifeboats. As was customary, women and children were loaded first. It was now 12:45 A.M., about one hour after the *Titanic* had struck the iceberg.

Nearby, the ship the *Californian* was at a full stop, its progress blocked by the massive field of ice in which the *Titanic* was trapped. On the deck of the *Californian*, crewmen reported to their captain that they had seen flares in the distance. The captain of the *Californian* ordered his crew to try to contact the distressed ship with a Morse lamp. They received no response from the *Titanic*. Meanwhile, the radio operator of the *Californian*, whose shift was over, was asleep in bed. No one on board the *Californian* had thought to wake him up. The "SOS" calls from the *Titanic* went unanswered by the *Californian*.

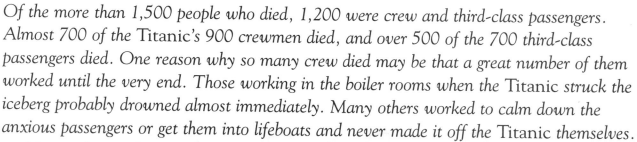

DID YOU KNOW . . .

most of those who died were crew and third-class passengers?

Of the more than 1,500 people who died, 1,200 were crew and third-class passengers. Almost 700 of the Titanic's 900 crewmen died, and over 500 of the 700 third-class passengers died. One reason why so many crew died may be that a great number of them worked until the very end. Those working in the boiler rooms when the Titanic struck the iceberg probably drowned almost immediately. Many others worked to calm down the anxious passengers or get them into lifeboats and never made it off the Titanic themselves.

No one knows for sure why so many third-class passengers died. There is speculation that crewmen kept third-class passengers locked down below in order to keep the decks less crowded, or to let first- and second-class passengers on the lifeboats first. It is also possible that many drowned before ever reaching the deck, because the third-class passengers' cabins were so far below the deck of the ship.

Back on the *Titanic*, the first lifeboats were being lowered into the water. They could carry sixty-five people, but they left with fewer than half that number. On deck, the passengers seemed to be relatively calm despite everything that was going on around them. However, as fewer and fewer lifeboats were left, passengers began to panic. Boats began filling up more rapidly; some left with more people than was regulated. Below deck, in the third-class areas, there was much more confusion. Gates to the upper decks were closed and may have been locked to avoid overcrowding the upper decks. Many third-class passengers could not get to where the lifeboats were. The frantic crowds scrambling to get to the upper decks crushed some of the weaker passengers. Others drowned in the hallways as water began filling the middle decks.

One of the crowded Titanic *lifeboats is hoisted aboard the rescue ship* Carpathia, *on April 15, 1912.*

19

By 2:00 A.M., the bow of the *Titanic* was completely underwater. More than 1,500 people were still on board—no lifeboats were left. Passengers began crowding the stern, some hoping for a miracle to occur. The weight of the bow pulled the propellers completely out of the water. The ship could not support the weight of the stern being lifted so high. Suddenly, there was a loud explosion as the *Titanic* began to split in two! It split between the third and fourth smokestacks. The bow began to drop to the bottom of the ocean, more than two miles down. The force of the split pulled the stern into a vertical position, its rear end pointed directly toward the midnight sky. It bobbed up and down in the water a few times, then descended quickly into the sea. It landed almost 2,000 feet away from the bow. Both pieces of the ship slammed into the bottom with such force, it is assumed they can never be removed from the ocean floor.

In the lifeboats, the survivors waited for help. They listened to the cries of those in the freezing water who did not make it onto a lifeboat. They watched for any signs of rescue. They prayed for those who had not made it and for their own safety. Two hours later, at about 4:00 A.M., the *Carpathia* reached the site where the *Titanic* had sunk. It managed to rescue only 705 of the more than 2,200 passengers on board the *Titanic*.

Corbis-Bettmann

The Carpathia *docked in New York City, after bringing back the* Titanic *survivors. Third-class survivors are still on board.*

Because of the *Titanic* disaster, new regulations regarding ship safety were adopted. These reforms include having enough lifeboat space for everyone on board, the regular practice of life jacket and lifeboat drills, the maintenance of a full-time radio watch, and the creation of the International Ice Patrol, which warns ships of dangerous, icy areas in the North Atlantic.

*This eerie photo, taken in 1991, shows the "rusticle"-encrusted bow of
the Titanic looming from the darkness of the Atlantic Ocean.*

AP/Wide World Photos

"THE UNSINKABLE SHIP"

"The Unsinkable Ship" was one of the many nicknames newspapers around the world gave the *Titanic*. Others included "the Millionaire's Special," "the Wonder Ship," "the Floating Palace," and "the Last Word in Luxury."

 Begin the *Titanic* by drawing two long, thin rectangles, the smaller on top of the larger.

 Add the four large smokestacks. Begin to shape the stern (back) and bow (front) of the ship.

3 Erase unneeded lines at the rear and front of the ship. Sketch three levels inside the top rectangle, and add the short vertical guidelines. Begin to detail the deck of the ship with shallow scooped shapes on either side.

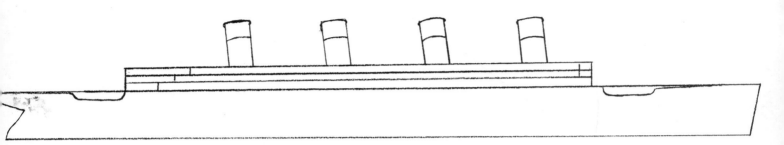

 4 Erase unnecessary lines at the edges of the top three levels and on the main deck. Add a fourth level underneath the three top levels by drawing a horizontal line across the length of the ship, just below the deck. Draw the porthole and the two masts, as well as guidelines for the lifeboats.

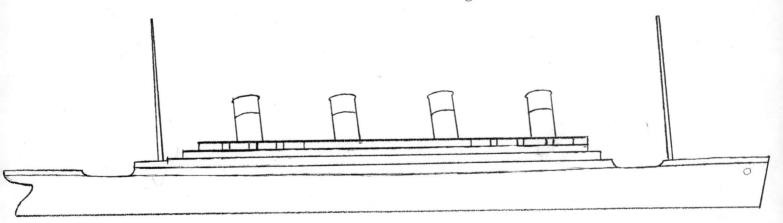

5 Erase unneeded lines along the top deck to create the lifeboats. Continue to detail the upper decks as shown.

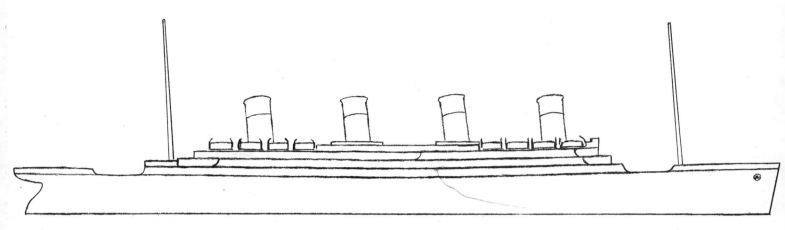

 6 Add the ropes and cables attaching the masts to the ship, including the lines from the smokestacks to the upper deck. Begin to add the windows to the upper decks.

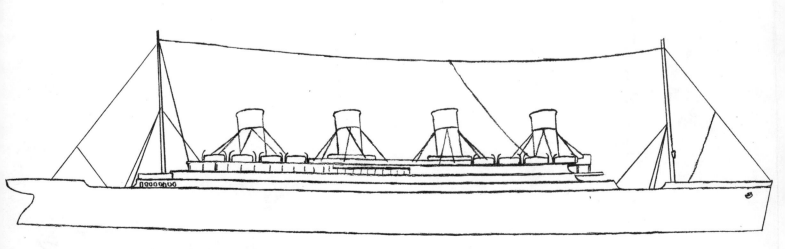

To complete the *Titanic*, draw the remaining windows across the upper decks. Darken in the windows, the hull of the ship, and the tops of the smokestacks. Use hatching to lightly shade the lower portion of each smokestack.

stern

hull

bow

DID YOU KNOW . . .
the *Titanic* disaster may have been predicted fourteen years earlier?

In 1898, Morgan Robertson, an American author, wrote a book that features the Titan, an enormous ship similar to the Titanic. Called "unsinkable," it sets sail from England to New York carrying many wealthy and famous people. The Titan sinks after hitting an iceberg in the middle of the Atlantic Ocean. Many of the Titan's passengers die because there are not enough lifeboats on board. Robertson's book was an eerie prediction of what happened to the Titanic fourteen years later.

CAPTAIN EDWARD J. SMITH

Captain Edward J. Smith was the commander of the R.M.S. *Titanic*. After loading the lifeboats with women and children, he is said to have told his crew, "Men, you have done your full duty. You can do no more. Abandon your cabin. Now it is every man for himself." Captain Smith and many of his crew went down with the *Titanic*.

 Draw an oval for Captain Smith's head and the guideline to show the center of his face. Add the guideline for his torso.

 Form the neck and shoulders. Draw guidelines for his eyes, nose, and mouth.

3 Now erase the guideline in his torso and down the center of his face. Draw the collar of his coat. Add the facial features as shown, including his ear, eyes, nose, and mouth. Begin his beard by drawing the mustache. Start to form the brim and top of his cap.

4 Erase unneeded lines around his head and face. Finish his cap, beard, and ear. Add structure to his face by forming his cheekbones. Draw the collar of his shirt, and begin to detail his coat.

5 Draw a large oval frame around Captain Smith. Continue detailing his beard, mustache, and clothing. Add his tie, coat buttons, and medals.

6 Finish your drawing by darkening his coat and cap. Lightly shade in his coat collar and face.

DID YOU KNOW . . .

Captain Smith may have overestimated the strength of the *Titanic?*

In 1911, Captain Smith commanded the Titanic's nearly identical sister ship, the Olympic. The naval cruiser Hawke rammed the Olympic, punching a 20-foot-wide hole in the starboard side. Although the Hawke was very badly damaged, the passengers aboard the Olympic were not even aware that there had been a collision. Based on this accident, Smith may have believed that these giant ships were truly "unsinkable."

A First-Class Female Passenger, Boarding

It was very important for the wealthy and famous to dress according to their status in society. First-class passengers would of course look at each other as they boarded the ship, so they took care to dress well. As pictured here, women of the time often wore large hats and carried umbrellas to guard against harmful sun rays.

 Begin your boarding female passenger by drawing an oval shape for her head. Add the guidelines for her torso, arms, and legs.

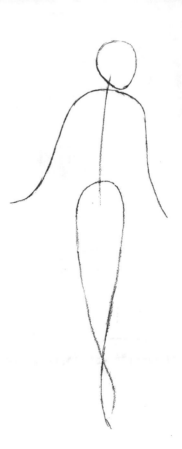

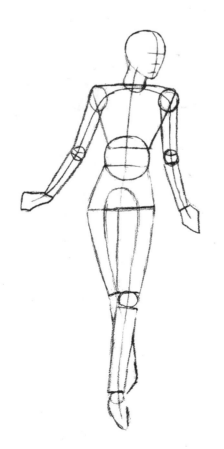

 Sketch the guidelines needed to draw her face. Using the guidelines, add her neck and rectangular shapes for her torso, arms, and legs. Draw circles for her joints and stomach. Add her hands and feet as shown.

3 Begin her facial features and hat. Extend her neckline out to her shoulders, and start to form her dress. Erase unneeded guidelines. Add details to her hands and shoes.

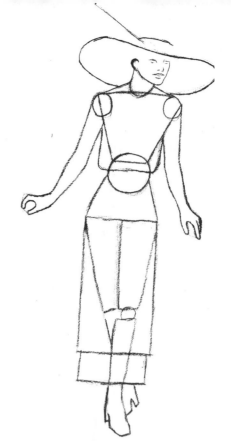

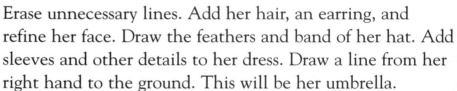

4 Erase unnecessary lines. Add her hair, an earring, and refine her face. Draw the feathers and band of her hat. Add sleeves and other details to her dress. Draw a line from her right hand to the ground. This will be her umbrella.

5 Finish detailing her dress—add the belt and a few folds in the material and along the hemlines. Complete her umbrella.

 Bring your female passenger to life by shading her hat, umbrella, and dress with light and dark pencil strokes. Darken her shoes, the feathers in her hat, and other details as shown.

DID YOU KNOW . . .

many first-class passengers brought their servants along for the trip?

Many first-class passengers wanted the trip to be as restful as possible. Therefore, they bought tickets for their maids, valets, and nannies to take care of the luggage, clean the rooms, or watch the children. Had the families in first class not paid for their workers to go, most of the servants would never have been able to travel on the Titanic.

A 1911 DELAGE AUTOMOBILE

Many wealthy passengers bought automobiles while they were traveling throughout Europe. The *Titanic* was bringing several of these automobiles back to the United States. This picture is of a 1911 Delage, a very popular car of the time.

 Begin your automobile by drawing two cube shapes, one much larger than the other. This is the basic body of the car.

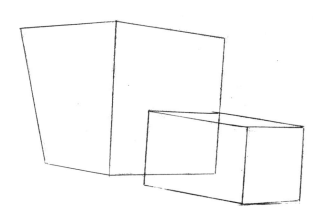

 Erase unneeded lines. Draw three circles for the wheels. (The fourth can't be seen.) On the front of the automobile, shape a triangular grille. Add the curved lines above the wheels for the guards. Draw lines across the larger cube shape for the door and windshield.

3 Complete the outline of the wheel guards. Add the canopy to the roof of the automobile. Draw the axle, extending from one front wheel to the other. Create the curved line for the bottom of the door. Add curved lines to the smaller cube to form the hood. Erase unneeded lines.

4 Further detail the wheels. On the inside of the grille, draw a square. Add circles for the headlights, steering wheel, and side-view mirrors. Draw two diagonal lines from the canopy to the wheel guards, and one line from the canopy to the top of the door. Begin to add details to the front end, and finish the running board as shown. Continue to erase unneeded lines.

5 Draw lines for the visible door. Complete the canopy by outlining the diagonal lines as shown. Add squares for windows in the rear and on the driver's side. Detail the running board and below the passenger door. Draw the radiator cap above the grille. Further detail the steering wheel, front end, and headlights as shown.

6 Form the spokes on the wheels. Detail the headlights and mirrors. Add the horn on the driver's side. Continue to detail the front end, hood, and doors.

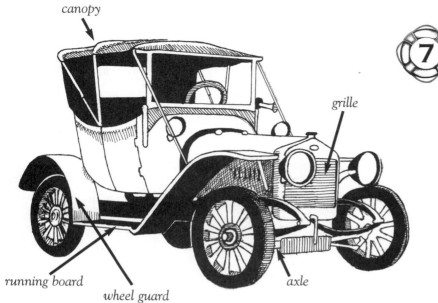

canopy

grille

running board

wheel guard

axle

7 Complete your automobile by darkening the area around the headlights, mirrors, and wheels, as well as the inside of the canopy and the underside of the wheel guards. To give your automobile a shaded effect, add hatching to the side of the car, below the wheel guards and the window, to the canopy, and to the inside of the wheels. Draw horizontal lines across the grille to detail it further. Color the automobile as you desire.

DID YOU KNOW . . .
a nearly intact automobile lies among the wreckage?

A Renault town car, a popular French automobile, is among the Titanic's wreckage. While it once belonged to a wealthy passenger, the car now lies at the bottom of the ocean, its bronze fixtures polished to a shine by the seawater.

A First-Class Female Passenger, About to Dine

Many first-class guests would meet in the reception room before dinner, where the women always wore their best gowns and jewels, and the men wore their formal wear. They would then go to the first-class dining saloon to feast on such foods as lobster, roast beef, and shrimp. Often, the Captain dined with his first-class guests.

 Begin your female diner by drawing an oval for her head. Add a guideline for the center of her face, as well as guidelines for her torso, arms, and legs.

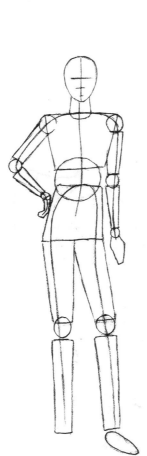

 Draw the guidelines for her eyes, nose, and mouth. Add her neck and rectangular shapes for her torso, arms, and legs. Draw circles for her joints and stomach. Add her hands and her left foot as shown.

MORTON COUNTY LIBRARY
Mandan, North Dakota

3 Draw her facial features and hair. Erase unneeded guidelines. Extend her neckline out to her shoulders. Sketch the guidelines for her dress sleeves, then begin her dress. Further detail her hands.

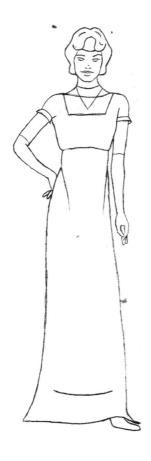

4 Erase unneeded lines. Finish the outline of her gown, and add lines for her necklace. Begin to sketch the front of her dress.

5 On her chest, erase lines as shown to create a collarbone. Detail her jewelry and headband, and further detail the skirt of her gown as shown.

 To create the smooth look of her gown, use the side of your pencil. Finish the female passenger by shading her dress and body. Darken her hair, facial features, and other details as shown. Leave her gloves white.

DID YOU KNOW . . .

there was an outdoor French café on board the *Titanic*?

One of the more popular places to eat among the first-class passengers was the Café Parisienne. It looked just like a French sidewalk café, with wicker chairs, potted plants, and ivy growing up the walls. Guests could enjoy pastries or other desserts and fine coffees at almost any time of the day or night.

A First-Class Male Passenger

Many wealthy men were on board the *Titanic*. John Jacob Astor, probably the world's richest man at the time, and George Widener, who made his fortune building streetcars, paid huge amounts of money to sail on "the Last Word in Luxury."

 Begin the male passenger by drawing a circle for his head. Add guidelines for his torso, arms, and legs.

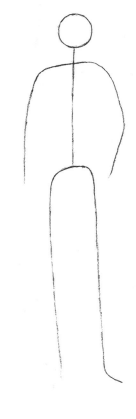

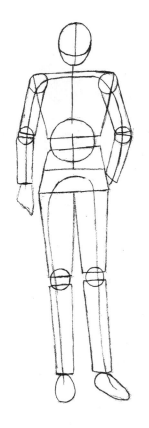

 Outline his chest and pelvic area. Draw rectangles to outline his arms and legs. Add circles for his joints and stomach as shown. Create guidelines for his facial features. Add shapes for his hands and feet.

3 Erase unneeded guidelines. Draw the lines at the top of his head for his hat. Add the guidelines for his eyes, nose, and mouth. Draw two lines from either side of his neck to his shoulders as shown. Begin to draw his coat and vest. Detail his right hand and his shoes. Draw a line for his cane.

4 Detail his hat and shoes. Add his eyes, ears, nose, and mouth. Erase unneeded guidelines. Continue the outline of his coat, and add his coat and shirt collars. Sketch lines to create the pocket and folds of his pants. Outline his cane.

5 Erase any remaining guidelines. Further detail his facial features. Draw his tie, the buttons and opening of his vest, and the band on his hat. Add the folds in his coat, and complete the outline of his coat and its collar. Draw the handle of his cane, and sketch squiggly lines on his shoes.

 6 Finish your illustration by coloring in his clothing and shoes as shown. Shade the top of his face just below his hat to create a shadowed effect. Leave areas of white as shown to create highlights throughout your drawing.

DID YOU KNOW . . .

the inventor of wireless communication survived the disaster?

One of the most important inventors in history, Guglielmo Marconi, survived the Titanic disaster. An Italian electrical engineer and Nobel Prize winner, he is most famous for inventing the first radio-signaling system. By means of an antenna, his system was able to send signals clear across the Atlantic Ocean, a feat only dreamed of by other engineers. Marconi's communications system was aboard the Titanic and was used to signal the Carpathia.

A CREWMAN

Crewmen worked around the clock shoveling coal into the 15-foot-high boilers. These boilers produced the steam that ran the *Titanic*'s engines. The engines, in turn, worked the propellers.

 Begin the crewman by drawing a circle for his head. Add guidelines for his torso, arms, and legs.

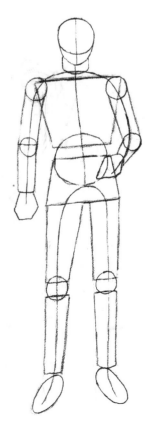

 Outline the sections of his body and limbs. Add circles for his joints and stomach as shown. Draw the guideline for his facial features. Add his neck, hands, and feet.

3 Erase unneeded guidelines. Draw the curved rectangle at the top of his head for his cap. Add guidelines for his eyes, nose, and mouth. Draw two lines from either side of his neck to his shoulders. Add the flaps and sleeves of his coat. Detail his hands and shoes. Add the outline of his glove and the small wrinkle in his pants. Create the curved line that will be the bottom of his shirt.

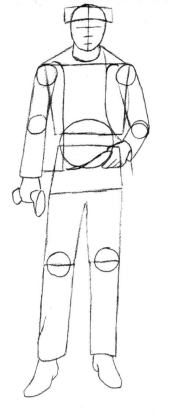

 4 Detail his cap and shoes. Add his eyes, ears, nose, mouth, and mustache. Erase unneeded guidelines. Draw the hair behind his ears and a small line in his chin. Add his coat collar and the wrinkle in his left sleeve. Create the fingers of his glove.

 5 Erase unneeded guidelines. Add the folds in his cap, and draw more folds in his shirt and pants. Detail the collar of his shirt. Add squiggly lines to his shoes.

Finish your crewman by coloring in his clothing. Notice he is only holding one glove; he is wearing the other one. Shade a little darker around the wrinkles in his clothing. This will add a three-dimensional, shadowed effect. Also leave some areas white for highlights.

DID YOU KNOW . . .

of the more than 900 crew on board the *Titanic*, only a little over 200 survived?

Half the crew worked in catering and domestics; the other half worked the mechanics of the ship. Despite the danger and the panic around them, the crew worked until the very last moment. Many crewmen drowned in the engine rooms very soon after the Titanic struck the iceberg. Some worked to clear the lower decks of people, while the rest tried to keep the nervous passengers calm.

A LIFEBOAT

Because the *Titanic* was thought to be unsinkable, only twenty lifeboats were attached to the ship. Together, these twenty lifeboats could hold a maximum of 1,200 people—just about half the number of passengers and crew who were on the *Titanic*. Had the ship been carrying the maximum number of people it was able to carry, barely one-third of them would have fit on the lifeboats.

 Begin your lifeboat by drawing a large rectangle.

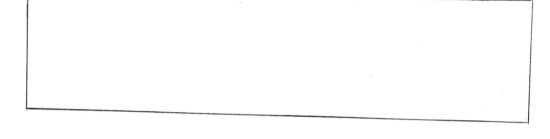

 Inside the rectangle, draw the pointed oval shape as shown. From either end of the oval, draw a diagonal line to the bottom of the rectangle. Add a curved line just below the bottom of the rectangle as shown. (This curved line should be parallel with the bottom line of the oval.)

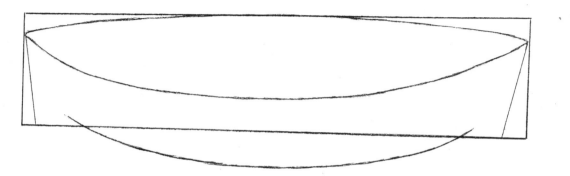

44

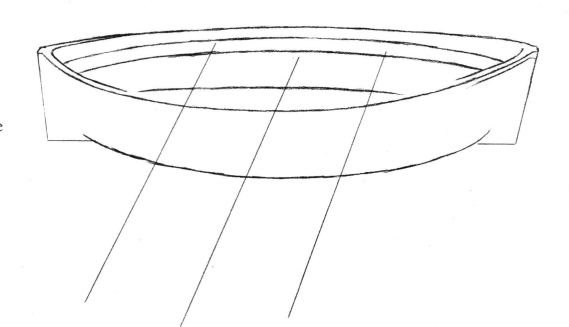

3 Erase the unneeded rectangular guidelines. Begin to draw the inside of the lifeboat by adding curved lines inside the oval as shown. Add three long, straight lines for the oars.

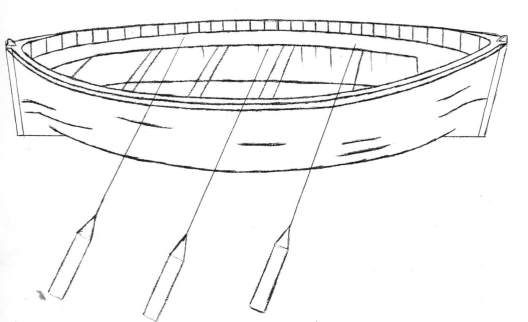

4 Add the lines for planks inside the boat—these will be the seats. Further detail the inside and outside of the lifeboat. Add paddles to the oars.

5 Erase unneeded lines inside the lifeboat, and finish outlining the oars. Further detail the hull and inside of the lifeboat as shown.

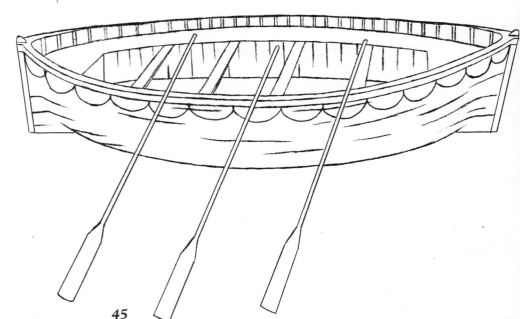

6 Darken the outer rim of the boat as shown. Finish your lifeboat by shading, using the hatching technique. This will give the lifeboat the appearance of wood.

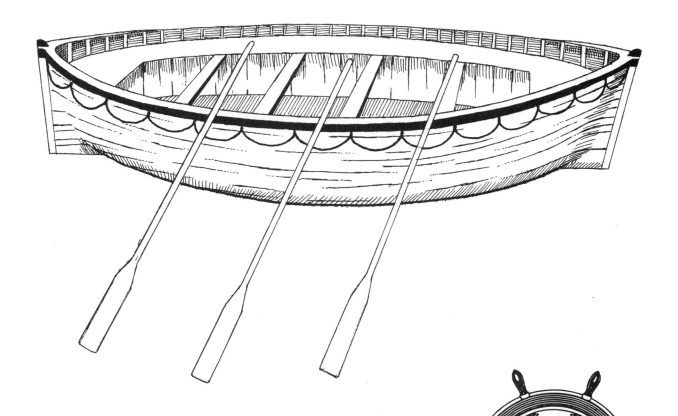

DID YOU KNOW . . .

only fourteen of the *Titanic's* twenty lifeboats were found?

The Carpathia began to recover thirteen lifeboats and 705 passengers at about 4:00 A.M. on Monday, April 15, 1912, a little more than an hour after the Titanic had completely sunk. The crew aboard the Carpathia were shocked to find that more than half of the lifeboats were less than half full with people. The Titanic's sister ship, the Olympic, discovered a fourteenth lifeboat almost one month later about 230 miles from the site of the sinking. The three bodies that were found aboard were buried at sea, and the lifeboat was sunk.

THE CARPATHIA

The *Carpathia* was the first ship to come to the rescue of the *Titanic*. It received a distress call soon after the *Titanic* had struck the iceberg, and it sailed at full steam through dangerous seas sprinkled with icebergs. Four hours after receiving the *Titanic*'s calls for help, the *Carpathia* arrived and was able to rescue 705 people. During World War I, it was torpedoed by a German submarine and it sank.

 Begin your illustration of the *Carpathia* by drawing a long rectangular shape. Make sure one end is a little wider than the other.

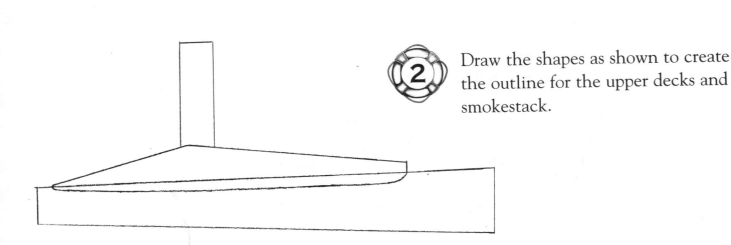 Draw the shapes as shown to create the outline for the upper decks and smokestack.

3 Begin to draw the guidelines for the different levels. (Curve the front ends of the different levels as shown to add a three-dimensional effect to your illustration.) Begin to shape the stern and bow, and detail the smokestack.

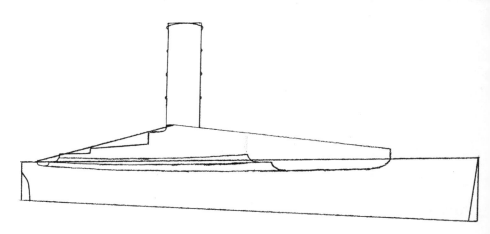

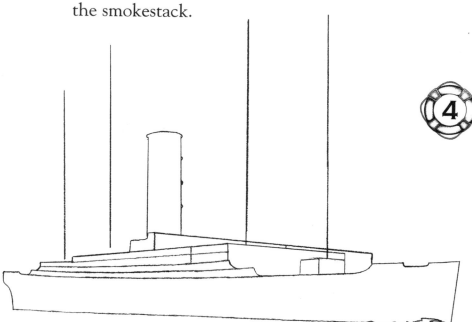

4 Erase unneeded lines at both ends of the ship and on the top levels. Add the scooped shapes near the bow and at the stern of the ship and the cubed shape near the bow. Sketch the four vertical lines for the masts. Draw more guidelines for the different levels. Add the crest of water near the bow.

5 Complete the smokestack as shown. Erase *and* add lines to create the lifeboats on the top deck. Complete the masts by drawing in the vertical lines. Add more guidelines on the different levels to create the decks. Draw the windows and porthole, as well as the V-shaped poles. Add the rectangular and triangular shapes to the top of the bridge.

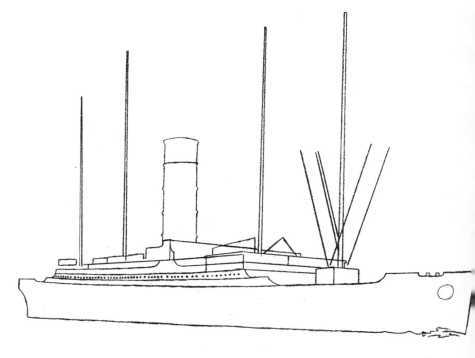

6 Draw the lifeboat supports and the crow's nest. Add horizontal lines to the deck just below the smokestack. Draw the windows of the bridge, and complete the figures on the top of the bridge (two lifeboats and a spool shape).

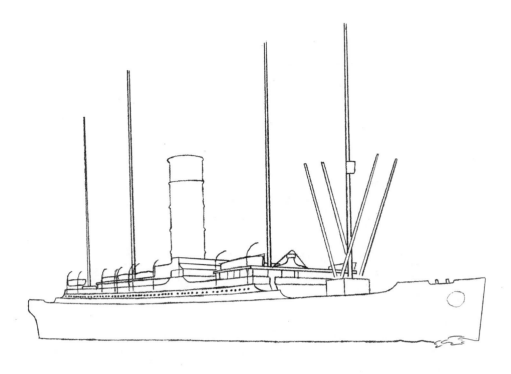

7 Erase unnecessary lines, and further detail the ship as shown. Add the cables from the tops of the masts and those from the smokestack to the deck. Don't forget to include the funnel, the anchor, and the guard rail at the front of the ship.

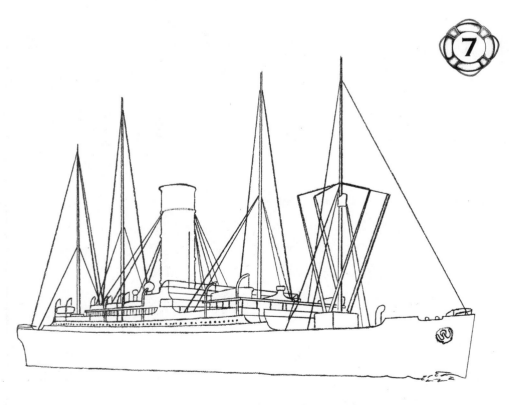

8 To complete the ship, darken the boat's hull and windows and the top of its smokestack. With light hatching, shade the side of the boat and smokestack. Add more cable from the masts to the ship's deck. Finally, sketch wispy smoke coming from the smokestack.

crow's nest

bridge

stern

bow

DID YOU KNOW . . .

"SOS" was not the original Morse code distress call?

Despite popular belief, "SOS" does not mean "Save Our Ship." The original Morse code distress call was "CQD." It was used by ships at sea to call for help. At the time of the Titanic disaster, "SOS" was just beginning to be widely used by ships, because it was much easier to translate than the "CQD" code. Take a look at the difference below.

S	O	S		C	Q	D
• • • /	– – – /	• • •	**or**	– • – • /	– – • – /	– • •

THE SUBMARINE *ALVIN*

Alvin, the tiny titanium submarine, is named after the oceanographer Al Vine. It is able to dive to 13,000 feet below sea level. Three people squeezed into *Alvin* in order to explore the wreckage of the *Titanic.* Attached to the sub was a self-propelled underwater robot named *Jason Junior.* Equipped with lights and cameras, "JJ" was able to record many of the pictures of the *Titanic* now available.

 1 Begin *Alvin* by drawing a quadrilateral shape.

2 Add two smaller four-sided shapes to the top and right of the original shape. Draw a curved line on the left. This will be the rear of the sub.

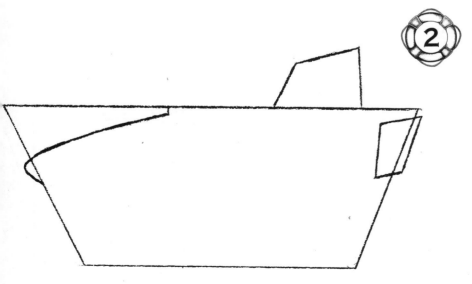

3 Erase the top-left corner and the unneeded line in the small shape on the right. Add the line to the topmost shape as shown. Draw a horizontal line across the middle of the original shape. Just above this horizontal line, draw a rectangle. To the right of the rectangle, draw the triangles as shown. Draw a curved line below the horizontal line. Create a small square in the bottom-left corner.

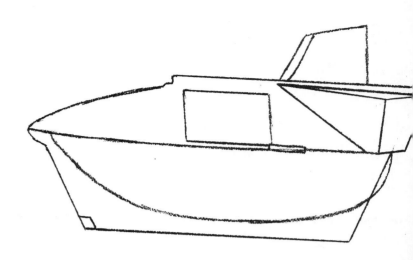

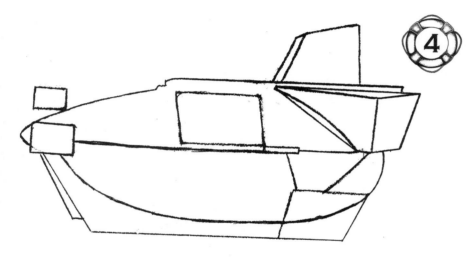

4 Draw two squares to the left of the original shape. Starting from the small square at the bottom left, draw a line up to the bottom of the large square to create a triangle shape as shown. Erase unneeded lines. Draw a large square in the bottom-right corner of the original shape. Add lines to form a quadrilateral above the square you just drew.

5 Erase unneeded lines. Draw the curved vertical line near the front of the ship. Sketch the thrusters inside the boxes on the left side of the sub. Directly in front of the shape at the top-right of the sub, draw the video camera. Below the camera, inside the original shape, create the oval shape as shown. Draw the oval viewport in the lower right of the sub. Near the center of the sub, below the horizontal line, draw two vertical lines. To the right of the sub, add the different shapes as shown.

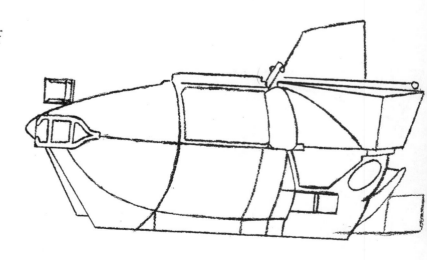

6 Erase any unneeded lines. Detail the top and bottom halves of the sub as shown.

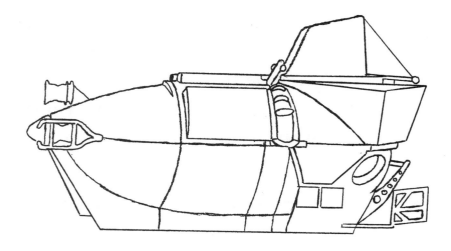

video camera

thrusters

7 To finish *Alvin*, blacken the areas shown. Then use the hatching technique to shade the underside and top of the submarine.

viewport

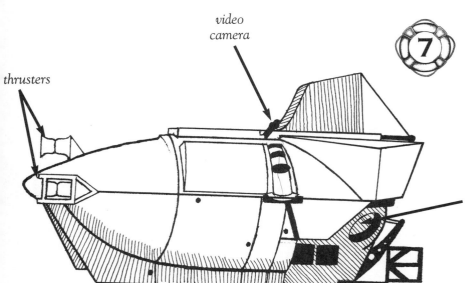

DID YOU KNOW . . .

Alvin has had a very long career?

In 1968, the United States Navy used Alvin to explore underwater volcanoes off the coast of New York. It has been used to study underwater fossils, mountain ranges, reefs, and other marine life, including the "famous" Project FAMOUS—French-American Mid-Ocean Undersea Study. Alvin has been used for more than thirty years and is booked for more studies in the future.

A TIGER SHARK

The waters of the Atlantic Ocean, where the *Titanic* is located, are home to many different types of marine life. Although the tiger shark won't be found in waters as deep as the *Titanic*'s location, it is one type of fish that may inhabit the Atlantic Ocean.

 Begin your illustration by drawing a large elongated oval.

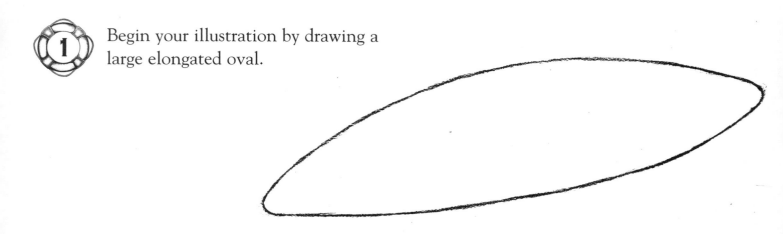

Add a half-oval to the left of the main shape to create the tail. Near the tail, add the curve to the body as shown, and extend the lines into the tail.

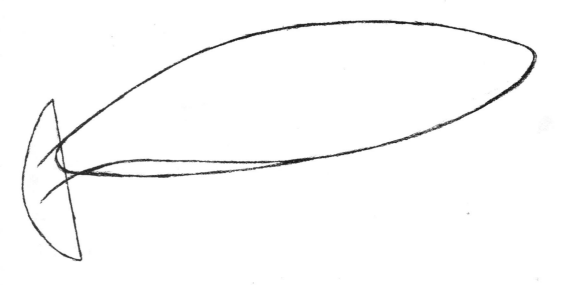

3 Erase the unneeded guideline from the oval. Add the fins and the detail of the tail. Begin the mouth, and draw the streamlined snout.

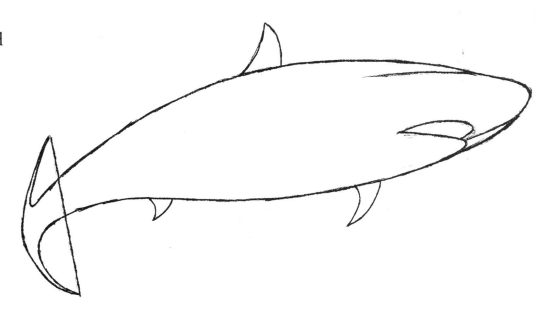

4 Erase the unneeded guidelines at the tail and snout. Draw a line from the top of the tail to the bottom tip. Add the fourth fin to the middle of the body. Draw the curving line from the snout to the tail to show the underside of the shark. Don't forget to add the tiny fifth and sixth fins near the tail, as well as the gills and eye.

5 Erase unneeded lines near the tail. Begin to detail your tiger shark by adding the stripes as shown. Further detail the line that shows the underside of the shark.

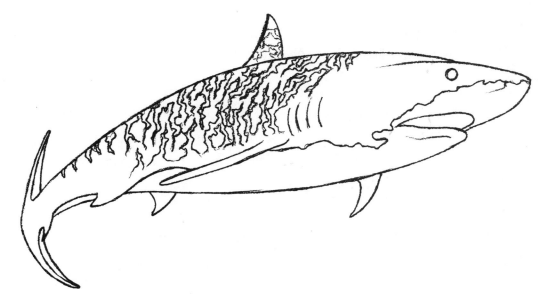

This tiger shark was detailed with stippling, a techniqe that uses dots instead of lines. Place the dots loosely on its underside and nose for light shading. Place them closer together on its top and sides, making the stripes darker. Fill in its eye and mouth.

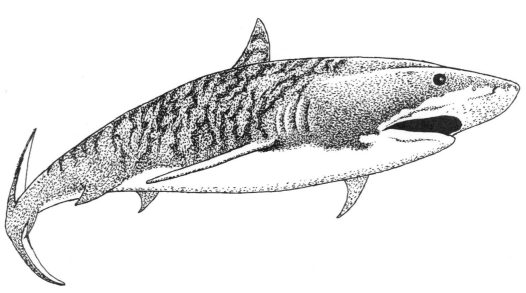

DID YOU KNOW . . .
the record depth a manned submarine has reached is about 35,000 feet?

In 1960, Jacques Piccard reached the record depth in the Mariana Trench, off the coast of Guam, in the tiny sub Trieste. At that depth, the water temperature is well below freezing. It is impossible to see, and no marine life can survive because sunlight cannot penetrate that deep. At 12,460 feet, the depth of the Titanic wreckage, it is difficult to see more than a few yards without very powerful lights. The water temperature is well below freezing, and water pressure measures 6,000 pounds per square inch.

A SWORDFISH

Divers aboard *Alvin* have had many close encounters with sharks and other fish. Fortunately, two inches of metal separates the divers from any danger. However, the fish haven't always been so lucky. According to Robert Ballard, on one trip aboard *Alvin*, a swordfish swam up to the sub to investigate. Apparently, it tried to attack *Alvin* and got its sword stuck right in the sub!

 Begin your swordfish by drawing an elongated oval shape.

 Inside the oval, draw the curved line for the belly. Add a long line from the fish's snout for its sword.

3 Erase the unneeded line at the bottom. Add the fins and tail. From the tip of the sword, draw a line back to the fish's body. Use this line to form the mouth.

4 Erase unneeded lines. Begin to detail the face with an eye and gills. Detail the fins and around the mouth. These lines will help with shading later.

5 Further detail the mouth, eye, and gills as shown. Make the backs of the fins and tail more realistic by drawing in more jagged edges.

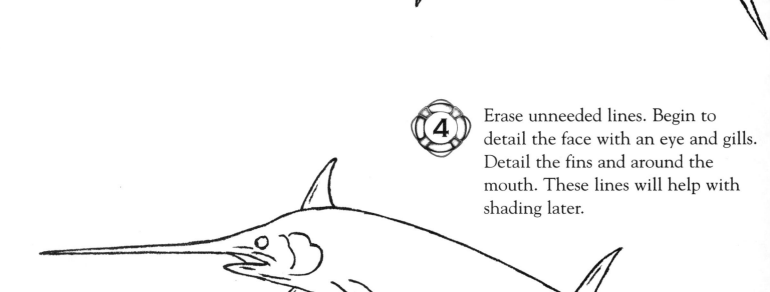

6 Complete your swordfish by using the stippling technique along the length of its body. Darken the tail, the undersides of the fins, and the inside of its mouth. To give a shadowed effect, add cross-hatching along the belly of the swordfish.

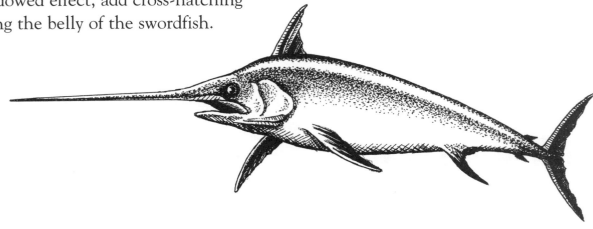

DID YOU KNOW . . .

a swordfish's "sword" isn't a sword at all?

The sword is actually an extension of its jawbone and can make up almost two-thirds of the body of a swordfish. The adult swordfish has no teeth, so it uses its "sword" to break up schools of fish and stun its prey before eating it. The sword is also used to scare off both fish and human predators. Swordfish is a very popular fish for food among humans.

When a hunter wounds a swordfish, the fish will often jump out of the water and thrash about, trying to wound its attacker. Sometimes it will pretend to be dead in order to draw the hunter closer. Then, when the hunter is very close, the swordfish will attack the hunter's boat, sticking its sword right into the hull!

TIPS ON COLOR

Your picture will stand out from the rest of the crowd if you use these helpful tips on how to add color to your masterpiece!

TRY WHITE ON BLACK

For a different look, try working on black construction paper or art paper. Then, instead of pencil, use white chalk, white pastel pencil, or poster paint. With this technique, you'll need to concentrate on drawing the light areas in your picture rather than the dark ones.

TRY BLACK AND WHITE ON GRAY (OR TAN)

You don't need special gray or tan paper from the art store for this technique. Instead, try cutting apart the inside of a grocery bag or a cereal box. This time, your background is a middle tone (neither light nor dark). Sketch your drawing in black, then use white to make highlights. Add black for the shadows.

TRY COLOR

Instead of using every color in your marker, colored pencil, or watercolor set, try using black for shadows, white for highlights, and one color for a middle tone. This third color blended with the white creates a fourth color. You will be surprised how professional your drawing will look.

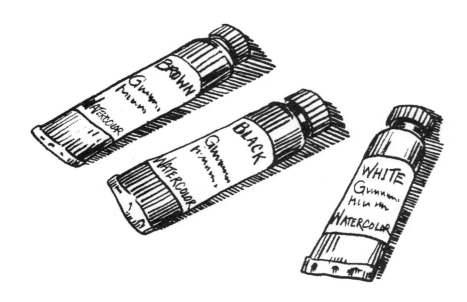

BACKGROUNDS

Once you have completed a drawing, you may want to put it in a setting. For example, you may want to put your drawing of the first-class diner in a restaurant, or the lifeboat in the ocean. Here are some suggestions for creating different settings.

MAGAZINE BACKGROUNDS

If you like to cut and paste, ask your family for some old magazines you can cut up. You can paste your drawing of the *Titanic* on an ocean scene that you cut out. Or, you may want to glue your character drawings onto a glamorous restaurant scene. You can also use fun magazine patterns to decorate your drawing. Just cut out pictures of different patterns and trim them so they're shaped like dresses or suits and paste them onto your characters.

PAINTED BACKGROUNDS

You don't need a paintbrush to add these painted backgrounds! To make small circles, dip the end of a straw into some paint and print the circles on your paper. You can make smaller circles by using the ends of tiny pieces of macaroni, or bigger ones with large macaroni. Cut a piece of sponge, dip it in paint, and stamp it on your picture to create the look of water. A crumpled piece of waxed paper or a paper towel can achieve the same effect. Be sure not to get these too wet, though, or they won't work well. Look around the house for other printing tools, such as old wooden spools, corrugated cardboard, or cut pieces of Styrofoam.

TEXTURED BACKGROUNDS

If you want to create a textured background, you'll need to draw the *Titanic* or a character on a thin piece of paper. Place a textured object (such as sandpaper) under the section of your paper where you want the texture to appear. Now grab a pencil with a soft lead. Then, using the side of the pencil lead, rub lightly and evenly over the area. For other cool textures, try using window screening, rough wood, a kitchen grater—anything you can imagine!

SHADOWED BACKGROUNDS

By adding shadows in the right places, your illustrations will leap off the page! Imagine where the shadow of the *Titanic* or a passenger would fall underneath the image. Then fill in those areas with a dark pencil. You might want to add shadows to some of the background scenery, too. When adding shadows to your backgrounds, remember that sunlight is different at different times of day. Morning and late-afternoon light make objects cast very long shadows. Whenever the sun is directly overhead, the shadows cast are very short.

GLOSSARY

aft: Toward the back of a ship.

boiler: A furnace in which coal is burned to boil water and create steam, which in turn drives the ship.

bow: The front end of a ship.

bridge: A raised platform or structure (usually enclosed), toward the front end of a ship, that has a clear view ahead and from which the ship is navigated.

crow's nest: A partly enclosed platform high on a ship's mast used as a lookout.

deck: A platform on a ship that serves as the floor for its compartments.

forward: Toward the front of a ship.

hold: A storage space for cargo on a ship, usually below decks.

hull: The frame or lower body of a ship that is partly below water when sailing.

iceberg: A large floating mass of ice detached from a glacier, most of which is underwater.

latitude: The distance, measured in degrees, north or south of the equator (0°).

longitude: The distance, measured in degrees, east or west of the prime meridian (0°) to the international date line (180°).

mast: A long pole rising from the deck of a ship that supports the ship's rigging.

Morse code: A system invented by Samuel Morse in which various combinations of dots and dashes stand for letters and numbers. Messages can be sent either by radio or by flashing lamp.

port: The left-hand side of a ship when facing the bow.

propeller: A device on a ship with radiating blades specially designed and placed so that when it turns it causes the ship to move forward.

ragtime: A style of music popular during the early part of the twentieth century.

rigging: Lines and chains used aboard a ship to work the sail and support the masts.

rivets: Pins or bolts of steel that hold metal plates together.

R.M.S.: Letters that stand for Royal Mail Steamer.

starboard: The right-hand side of a ship when facing the bow.

stern: The rear end of a ship.

telegraph: A machine, system, or process that sends electric signals over a wire to cause communication at a distance.

Turkish bath: A steam bath.

wheelhouse: The small covered area on the bridge of a ship where the ship's wheel is located. Also called the pilothouse.

wireless: An early form of radio.

Hulton Deutsch/Corbis